# Math Counts

# Pattern

Introduction

In keeping with the major goals of the National Council of Teachers of Mathematics Curriculum and Evaluation Standards, children will become mathematical problem solvers, learn to communicate mathematically, and learn to reason mathematically by using the series Math Counts.

Pattern, Shape, and Size may be investigated first—in any sequence.

Sorting, Counting, and Numbers may be used next, followed by Time, Length, Weight, and Capacity.

Ramona G. Choos, Professor of Mathematics, Senior Adviser to the Dean of Continuing Education, Chicago State University; Sponsor for Chicago Elementary Teachers' Mathematics Club

About this Book

Mathematics is a part of a child's world. It is not only interpreting numbers or mastering tricks of addition or multiplication. Mathematics is about ideas. These ideas have been developed to explain particular qualities such as size, weight, and height, as well as relationships and comparisons. Yet all too often the important part that an understanding of mathematics will play in a child's development is forgotten or ignored.

Most adults can solve simple mathematical tasks without the need for counters, beads, or fingers. Young children find such abstractions almost impossible to master. They need to see, talk, touch, and experiment.

The photographs and text in these books have been chosen to encourage talk about topics that are essentially mathematical. By talking, the young reader can explore some of the central concepts that support mathematics. It is on an understanding of these concepts that a child's future mastery of mathematics will be built.

Henry Pluckrose

1995 Childrens Press® Edition
© 1994 Watts Books, London, New York, Sydney
All rights reserved.
Printed in the United States of America.
Published simultaneously in Canada.
12 13 14 15 R 10 09 08 07 06 05 04

# Math Counts

# Pattern

By Henry Pluckrose

Mathematics Consultant: Ramona G. Choos,
Professor of Mathematics

CHILDRENS PRESS ®
CHICAGO

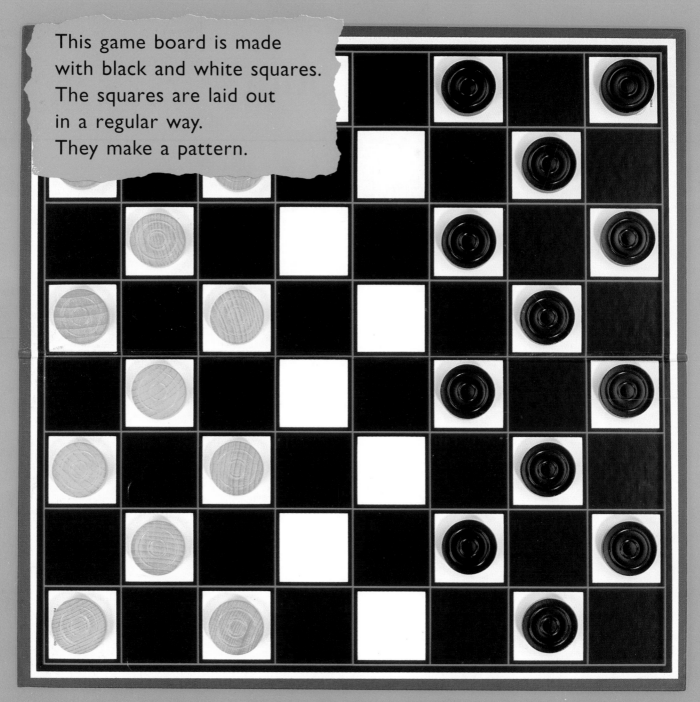

This game board is made
with black and white squares.
The squares are laid out
in a regular way.
They make a pattern.

4

This board also is made
with black and white squares.
They are not laid out in a regular way.
They do not make a pattern.

5

Patterns are all around us.
You can find patterns in nature—
on the heads and petals of flowers,

on leaves,

7

on birds,

and butterflies.
Is the pattern on each wing
of the butterfly exactly the same?

There is a spiral pattern on this shell

and a pattern of stripes
on the coat of the zebra.

We decorate our homes
with patterned wallpaper and fabric.

We put patterned carpets on the floor.

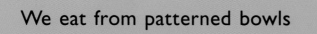

We eat from patterned bowls

14

and plates.

Things we wear
are often patterned,

16

and so are clothes
worn on special occasions.

Many patterns repeat themselves.
Can you see the repeat
in this pattern?

Some patterns repeat themselves
in a different way.
How does this pattern repeat itself?

There are patterns
almost everywhere.
What shapes repeat themselves
in these cranes to make a pattern?

What pattern can you see in these cobblestones?

21

Some shapes fit together tightly
to make a pattern

and some leave little spaces.
The spaces make a pattern too.

These swimmers are making a pattern with their bodies.

The water makes a circular pattern when a drop hits the surface.

This is a close-up of a car tire. Why does it have this pattern?

There is also a pattern on the sole of this shoe. How does the pattern stop a runner from slipping?

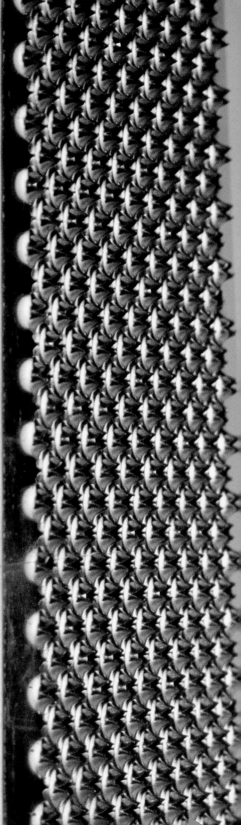

Why does this grater have a pattern?

28

The spiral pattern
on the rope
gives the climber
a good grip.

Look around you.

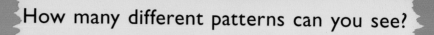

How many different patterns can you see?

Library of Congress Cataloging-in-Publication Data

Pluckrose, Henry Arthur.
   pattern / Henry Pluckrose.
    p.  cm.
   Originally published: London; New York: F. Watts 1988.
   (Math counts)
   Includes index.
   ISBN 0-516-05455-4
    1. Repetitive patterns (Decorative arts) — Juvenile literature. 2. Pattern perception — Juvenile literature.
   [1. Pattern perception.] I. Title.
   NK1570.P59  1995
   745.4 — dc20

                                          94-38008
                                          CIP
                                          AC

**Photographic credits:** Chris Fairclough, 4, 5, 6, 7, 9, 10, 11, 14, 15, 16, 18, 19, 20, 21, 23, 26, 27, 28, 29, 30, 31; © Walter Rawlings, 8; PhotoEdit © Michelle Bridwell, 12; Axminster Carpets Ltd., 13; Robert Harding Picture LIbrary, 17; Eye Ubiquitous © Roger Chester, 22; ZEFA, 24, 25

**Editor:** Ruth Thomson
**Design:** Chloë Chessman

# INDEX